GW00864985

Oyster Delight

by

Jonathan Mite

with

Illustrations by John Joyce

The definitive guide to enjoying oysters!

ISBN Number: 9781469999920

Oyster Delight

by

Jonathan Mite

with

Illustrations by John Joyce

Table of Contents

A word of welcome to the culinary bliss of consuming one of the world's greatest delicacies

Oysters have long been acclaimed to have the most wonderful effects on their consumer; and who are we to state otherwise. Archeologists are always finding

prehistoric kitchen middens (garbage dumps) littered with oyster shells. One of the things defining such middens is the presence of oyster shells. I suppose that even cave men knew what was good for them. In fact, oysters have been cultivated by man for more than 2000 years.

Kitchen Midden found in the west of Ireland

The continued love for oysters by our fellow men and women might even be construed to point to a natural selection of oyster eaters over those who don't ... so where would humanity be today without oysters?

My motto:
"Eat Oysters and Love Longer"

Oysters are delicious, especially fresh on the half-shell, but there are also many mouth-watering dishes you can prepare to increase your enjoyment even more. After many years happily trying out new recipes, I was finally persuaded to pass on some of my favorites.

Excerpted from the timeless treatise:

"The World According to Jonathan"

Fossilized Oyster Shells and Brachiopods from the Jurassic Period (200 – 140 million years ago) found by Meike Blackwell in 2007 near Kimmeridge in southern England.

1.   About the Author

Alex Blackwell, scribe and oysterman

Jonathan Mite was born in the ImagiNation™ a while back. I am not sure, when he first popped up, but it was through Jonathan that I penned the predecessor to this book. I wrote it for my family, friends and customers many years ago. You see, I was in the oyster business. I had a hatchery and a farm. I bought oysters from all over Ireland and shipped them off to oyster lovers in continental Europe. I also supplied the local restaurants with fresh oysters, striving to create a demand for what has since turned out to be a very popular culinary delight. When we decided that others might be interested in this book, we debated who was to receive credit as author.

Jonathan Mite,
His name just felt right,
He had helped me out,
When times were tight,
And his name rhymed,
With "Oyster Delight".

My first memory of oysters is being in an Alice in Wonderland play. All of us children had to stand around freezing on a chilly summer night. We then had to swim across a cold pool dressed up as oysters. It all ended when I was slurped by the walrus after which he tossed my shells into the heap. He was a happy walrus and he recited the following poem, which has stayed with me all these years:

A loaf of bread, the Walrus said,
Is what we chiefly need.
Pepper and vinegar besides
Are very good indeed –
Now, if you're ready, oysters dear,
We can begin to feed.

Lewis Carroll
from
Alice in Wonderland.

Since then I too have loved oysters!

2

2. Foreword

Daria Blackwell, editor and oyster gourmand

I was introduced to oysters as a young college student. I don't recall the first oyster I ate because it was quickly followed by a second, third, and fourth. How could a simple mollusk be so temptingly delightful on the palate?

Alex learned to love oysters in a different way – from the perspective of child growing up on the coast, and then as a scientist. You see, Alex is a marine biologist who fell so madly in love with oysters he had to share them with the world. So, in the 1980s, he started an oyster hatchery in Ireland, and promptly started delivering baby oysters to oyster farmers throughout Europe. You might consider him the father of whole colonies of delectable oysters that have now come of age and are ready for your enjoyment.

Alex knows a lot about oysters. He can tell one from another just by looking at them. Me, I have to taste them. Just pop one succulent little oyster in and let it slide gently down. Then I usually go for another, just to see if it's different. And so on, and so on, and so on. Lucky for me, oysters are good for you, especially at our home in the West of Ireland where the water is pure and the Guinness stout flows freely.

So we would like to share some of our experience with oysters with you.

Alex and I will give you some background on oysters along with a brief oyster-lover's description of the different varieties (makes it fun to experiment when you travel). Through Jonathan we will then share some of our favorite recipes... and oh, how delightful they are!

Bon appetite!

4

3.   What is an oyster?

An oyster is a bivalve mollusk. Just like a clam or a mussel, it has two shells protecting a soft body, which are characteristically thick and rough. Perhaps the most striking difference between oysters and their bivalve cousins (scallops, clams, mussels, etc) is their thick shell. It is this often sharp and wrinkly looking shell that can make an oyster quite difficult to eat.

Whereas a clam may bury itself into the sand or mud and move about, and a mussel has tremendously strong threads it uses to attach itself to solid objects, and is thus able to move as well, an oyster can never voluntarily change its position. Like all bivalves, it is a filter feeder. It pumps seawater past its gills, which also act similar to a very fine strainer. Any particles are taken out of the water. The food (microscopic algae) is sorted out and ingested, while the silt and sand are coated in mucus and excreted as mud so that it drops to the sea floor.

In a coastal area, where there is a lot of silt in the water, this leads to a rapid accumulation of sediment or just plain mud. This in turn fuels the popular misconception that oysters like to bury themselves in the mud. However, the reality is that if the mud is not washed away by wave action or a strong current, the oysters can become buried and will then die.

Bivalves are members of the mollusk family which also includes snails and squid. These are also soft-bodied animals. The snails (for the most part) have a single main shell with a smaller shell they use as a door and can close in times of danger. Most squid have an internal shell that gives their body a bit of rigidity.

The mollusk family

In the English language, for some reason all mollusks are grouped together with the crustaceans (crabs, lobsters and shrimp) into a group without any biological foundation called shellfish. In many regions 'shellfish' are therefore regulated as an entity.

The other main commercial grouping is fin-fish. These include salmon, cod, herring etc, etc as well as shark, dolphins and whales! Now shark are in reality a different family as their skeleton is made from cartilage and not bone. Then there are the dolphins and whales, which belong to the cetacean family. They are mammals and thus more closely related to us, than to actual 'fish'!).

To add to this confusing nomenclature, all marine animals are ganged together as "fish". So, if I refer to our delectable oyster as a fish, please forgive me...

All Kinds of Oysters

Oysters comprise a number of different groups of molluscs which grow for the most part in marine or brackish water. The "true oysters" are the members of the family Ostreidae. These include the edible oysters, which mainly belong to the genera Ostrea, Crassostrea, Ostreola and Saccostrea.

The native European oyster, *Ostrea edulis*, gets the common name "flat oyster" from its shell shape. The top shell is plate-like and flat, while the bottom shell is only slightly rounded. Although the flat oyster is the original native species for most of Europe, the British Isles, and the eastern coast of North America, they have since become quite scarce as they have been ravaged by disease.

Some delicious flat oysters (Ostrea edulis) from Clew Bay Ireland

The flat oysters generally have a lovely strong flavor and firm flesh. Because of their scarcity due to over fishing and disease, they fetch a comparatively high price and it is consequently a shame to cook them. We prefer to enjoy them raw.

Today so called "cupped oysters" account for most of what you will find on offer, particularly from farms. The *Crassostrea* species are known as cupped oysters on account of their deeper body form. Their shape is more elongated than *O.edulis*. The cupped oyster, which you can often have all year long, is usually a much plumper fish. It has a deliciously delicate almost creamy flavor. Being readily available in lager quantities, it lends itself both to cooking as well as eating raw.

Whereas *O. edulis* grows best in a full marine environment, some of the *Crassostrea* species thrive in both the marine and more brackish estuarine waters. Not only does this give them a greater area in which to grow, but the estuaries will often have a greater nutrient content. More nutrients mean more algae, which in turn speeds the oyster's growth.

Crassostrea gigas, which derives its name from the large size it can grow to, is now the most common oyster in Europe accounting for 75% of production. *C. gigas* is native to the Pacific coast of Asia – hence its common name Pacific Oyster. It has been introduced to North America, Australia, Europe, and New Zealand.

8

A fine example of Crassostrea gigas grown in Clew Bay Ireland

The other common species of the *Crassostrea* family are: *C. virginica* being common on the US Atlantic coast. Then you will find *C. commercialis* in Australia and New Zealand, *C. angulata* in Portugal and *C. eardelie* throughout the Philippines.

To make matters even more complicated, for each species, there are countless varieties stemming from different Bays or regions. Which type you prefer may be pretty much a matter of local taste and availability!

In Europe, you'll see major "discussions" arising about which is the best of the flat oysters. There are Colchesters, Whitstables, and many other varieties from England. Belons are the best known variety from France, and Tralee Bay, Galway Bay and Clew Bay are the main Irish varieties. Of course, our favorite is the Clew Bay oyster, but then we are slightly biased, as this is our home. In our humble opinion, there is no finer delicacy on earth than one of these strongly flavored morsels from the West of Ireland. The flavor and texture of each is affected by the quality of the water and local algae.

Naturally viable populations of flat oysters have appeared in eastern North America from Maine to

Rhode Island subsequent to artificial introduction in the 1940s and 1950s. Flat oysters are now also being farmed in the states of California, Maine, and Washington.

The same applies to the cupped oysters. For example, the East Coast of the United States sports well known varieties of the species *Crassostrea virginica* such as Chincoteagues from Chesapeake Bay, Blue Points from Long Island, and Wellfleets from Cape Cod, as well as many others.

In Puget Sound, the oyster beds have been seeded with many varieties of oysters and a favorite activity in Seattle is sampling all the different varieties available locally; including the native Olympia oyster *Ostreola conchaphila*, which, as you will note, belong to yet another different genus. What a great way to spend a lunch hour!

Oysters are produced pretty much everywhere in the world. I even spent a brief while working on an oyster research project in Israel, where oysters are not very popular, as they are not kosher.

When asked the direct question, I find it difficult to express a preference for one species or variety over the other. All are very nice, but each 'fish' is quite a different from the other. It's well worth trying them all and fueling the controversy! In fact, why don't you help us solve this timeless dilemma! Send us an email and tell us which is your favorite oyster.

And then, there are Pearl Oysters and Oyster Pearls

Pearl Oysters of the *Pinctada* genus occur over a wide area of the Pacific Ocean. In fact they are not related to the 'edible oysters' of the *Ostreidae* family, and they are harvested for their pearls and not for their meat.

However, on occasion, you may find a small pearl in a regular oyster. After all, a pearl is a natural phenomenon. You may even find them in mussels and other bivalves.

If a grain of sand finds its way into the space between the oyster's body and its shell, the oyster coats it with mother-of-pearl (calcium) in the same process as adding another layer to the inside of its shell. Usually the sand grain will get glued to the shell and will later just be another bump on the inside. However, sometimes this particle will roll around in the cavity, and the oyster will keep coating it with layer upon layer of material – eventually building up a visible pearl.

4.   Acquiring Oysters

Well, undoubtedly the best way to acquire oysters, is to walk a beach at low tide, collect a couple of dozen and open them then and there. If you are lucky, you will have access to an oyster bed. Now don't be thinking about your four-poster in your bedroom, though this is perhaps what inspired entrepreneurial oyster farmers with the contraptions they use to keep their livestock off the seafloor. An oyster bed is an area of beach that is firm enough for the oysters to lie on, has a good water flow over it (with water comes food), and is in an area where oysters can happily reproduce.

Traditionally wild oysters are dredged or scraped from the seabed where they live. There are many regional differences in how dredges are constructed, but generally there is a blade that is dragged over the bottom and a sack or cage to capture any object the blade might dislodge.

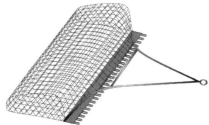

An oyster dredge will often have teeth to rake the seabed and a bag to collect the catch

More common nowadays is that the oysters are farmed. The small oysters are put into stiff mesh bags

13

which are held above the sea floor on metal frames or trestles. This keeps them from being buried in the mud and also allows them to grow a more even shell.

Working on oysters at Belon, Brittany, France - Photo by Peter Gugerell, 2005

Many oyster fishermen and farmers sell directly to the public, which makes for a pleasant outing to the local docks and is a great way to acquire really fresh fish.

If you do acquire your oysters from a fisherman, farmer or collect them yourself, why not plan in a picnic and consume them then and there! Just don't forget to bring along a couple of bottles of Guinness, some nice white wine or a bottle of Champagne to wash them down, as well as some fresh brown bread and butter. Nothing beats newly shucked, absolutely fresh oysters raw!

We are sailors and for us the ultimate in decadence is having oysters delivered to our boat while we swing at anchor somewhere in paradise. We first experienced this while cruising the East coast of the US. We were spending the evening in the outer harbor at Cuttyhunk in the Elizabeth Islands off Massachusetts when the raw bar boat came by selling locally farmed oysters shucked to order.

The Cuttyhunk Raw Bar Boat delivering oysters

straight from the local oyster beds

The next time was in the Caribbean in the Grenadines, where 'Roberto', paddled over and offered us mangrove oysters (*Crassostrea rhizophora*) – "They are small but oh so tasty". We shared a drink with him while he shucked the little morsels. And tasty they were indeed!

Fresh oysters, a nice bottle of wine, a fabulous sunset, the gentle swaying of our boat in the breeze... Now that is living!

Roberto with fresh mangrove oysters in Carriacou, Grenada

If you don't happen to live near a coast, don't despair. Just go and buy your oysters from a reputable fish merchant. Most people reading this book will be living in an area with a fast and modern shipping infrastructure, where fresh produce can be transported even to remote places and still be fresh.

Oysters can now also be ordered online through the internet and then shipped direct to your door from any number of sources throughout the world. You could even organize a global oyster feast at your home, by simply clicking your way to a sampling of several international varieties. Again, make sure you order from reputable dealers.

Freshness

Wherever you wind up acquiring your oysters, freshness is key! If you buy them at the fish market, or for that matter in the supermarket, here are a few things to look for. Fresh oysters should be closed really tight. They should be kept chilled, but not frozen, and never in stagnant water.

Never select any shellfish that are open; that usually indicates that the mollusk has gone bad. If you are going to cook the oysters, they may sometimes be open slightly. Test them by pressing the top of the shell near the opening. If the shell closes immediately, it's healthy and ready to go home to be cooked by you.

In some areas, oysters are available seasonally. The old rule for 'shellfish' is that any month containing the letter R (in the English language) is a good month. The months with an 'R' are the colder months. (Note: this rule only works for the Northern Hemisphere.) When the waters get warmer, bacteria content in inshore waters may increase and toxic algal blooms may occur, so safety restrictions may be enacted by the local fisheries authorities. In other areas, there may be no restrictions on when the oysters can be harvested. So, with a bit of caution and common sense, you may sample them year round.

Those of you who have to buy your oysters canned or in jars will do well with a good recipe for cooking them, so please do read on. To us, any way of having oysters is worthwhile; and if you're spared the work of shucking, why not?

Storage & Safe Handling

Oysters are live animals and consequently have a very limited "shelf life" once they've been taken out of the sea. As a rule you should purchase the oysters no more than two days in advance.

To keep them fresh for the maximum period, keep the oysters moist (but not wet) in a refrigerator or cold room at about 4 degrees Celsius (40 degrees F) prior to opening. Do not let them freeze unintentionally. Do not seal the container you have them in and always make certain that it does not have any water in it. If submersed for any length of time in anything but fresh flowing seawater, the oyster will die. You should also store the oysters with the flat side up. This way the oyster will not lose the moisture inside its shell and dry out.

The length of their shelf life also depends on a number of other factors which are out of your control but which you should still bear in mind. The most important factor (for a number of reasons) is that the oysters must come out of clean water. Pollution can greatly reduce the shelf life of an oyster, besides being very dangerous to the consumer. So, that brings you back to the question of where the oysters came from.

The oysters should also be shore-trained. Yes, the oyster needs training to stay closed! The muscle, which you must sever to open the oyster, must be trained to keep the shell closed firmly for a long period of time; something the oyster might not normally need to do. If not properly trained, the oyster will open up, lose the water out of its shell, dry up, and die.

If you think you may need to store them longer than a day or two, cook your remaining oysters and freeze them. You can later reheat them, and they will still be lovely. Several of the recipes offered here call for pre-cooked oysters and many others work with them as well.

Oyster Delight by Jonathan Mite

20

5.   Oysters and Sex

(This headline always gets attention)

Oysters have always been linked with love. When Aphrodite, the Greek goddess of love, sprang forth from the sea on an oyster shell and promptly gave birth to Eros, the word "aphrodisiac" was born.

A significant portion of the body of an oyster is devoted to its reproductive organs (male and female alike). This perhaps goes a way towards explaining the oysters' almost universal renown as an aphrodisiac. It may be important to note than Casanova is said to have consumed oysters daily to maintain his 'vigor'. There is even some scientific evidence indicating that oysters may indeed contain compounds that have been shown to be effective in releasing sexual hormones such as testosterone and estrogen. So, who am I to contradict this?

The other question that always crops up is the sex life of an oyster. I am not going to get into this here, as this may be a bit too raunchy for a cookbook – it is also really not all that exciting.

People used to also often ask me how I could tell a male oyster from a female. Whereupon I would explain (in jest) that the female's shell was much softer to the touch. This would usually buy me some peace and quiet, while the inquisitive mind tried to come to grips with a soft oyster shell...

Oysters are Good for You

A simple and true statement

Nutrition Facts
Serving Size 6 medium oysters (84.0 g)
Amount Per Serving

Calories 57		Calories from Fat 19
		% Daily Value*
Total Fat	2.1g	3%
Saturated Fat	0.6g	3%
Polyunsaturated Fat	0.8g	
Monounsaturated Fat	0.3g	
Cholesterol	45mg	15%
Sodium	177mg	7%
Total Carbohydrates	3.3g	1%
Protein	5.9g	
Vitamin A 2%		Vitamin C 5%
Calcium 4%		Iron 31%
Based on a 2000 calorie diet		

Also rich in vitamin B12, iron, zinc, and copper, oysters are thought to have regenerative and invigorating properties. All I know is that a dozen go down very well! And then there are the after-effects...

Good points

No sugar

Very high in iron

High in manganese

High in magnesium

High in phosphorus

Very high in selenium

Very high in vitamin B12

Very high in zinc

Bad points

High in cholesterol

High in sodium

6.   A Serious Note about Allergies

Yes, there are some poor people who are allergic to shellfish (mollusk) proteins. That is sadly a reality, and a crying shame. These poor people must miss enjoying one of life's delicacies.

As with other shellfish related allergies, symptoms can range from mild such as oral allergy syndrome to the severe such as anaphylactic shock. Seafood related allergies are the most common of all food allergies worldwide.

If someone has been diagnosed with an allergy to one mollusk, they will usually be advised by their physician to avoid all mollusks. On the other hand, people with a known allergy to shrimp can usually consume mollusks without reaction. However, there are rare cases where an individual is allergic to both types of 'shellfish'. Likewise, persons who are known to be allergic to finfish (such as cod or salmon) do not generally have allergies to shellfish (mollusks and crustaceans).

All shellfish allergies are primarily due to an individual's reaction to tropomyosin, a protein present in mollusks. Symptoms of an oyster or mollusk allergy are:

- Urticaria (hives) and angioedema (swelling)
- Urticaria (hives) of the hands from handling seafood
- Asthma
- Vomiting, loose stools and abdominal pains
- Mild to severe Atopic Eczema
- Anaphylaxis leading to the possibility of death

So yes, shellfish allergies must be taken very seriously! Call your doctor if you or someone else starts exhibiting allergic symptoms.

7.   How to get at the Goodies

If opening one of these tight-lipped delicacies has kept you from enjoying them at your leisure, fear no more. It's really quite simple. Whether you're looking for an elegant snack to set the mood or diving for pearls for that special someone, we'll help you master basic tricks for conquering this exquisite shellfish.

Open the oysters immediately before serving. Figure 1-2 minutes to open each oyster. Here are some things you might want to set up before starting:

Tools:

- A stiff brush
- At least one kitchen towel
- An oyster knife (see description below)
- A pail for shucked shells
- A heavy pair of gloves (optional, but advisable and will save your hands while you're learning)

Before you start opening your oysters, you should scrub them well and rinse them in clean, cold water. Never soak them in fresh water, because they can die if they open and their liquid drains out.

The Oyster Knife:

Oyster knives come in a wide variety of shapes and sizes. About the only common trait is that they have a fairly thick blade and are usually not sharp. Most oyster lovers will have more than one oyster knife. This is something one tends to collect over the years. Oysters are not the easiest thing to open so one is tempted to be on a lifelong quest for the perfect implement.

Shop for a good oyster knife at a good kitchen supply store, online, or at your local fish market. Strength and durability are more important than sharpness or size. It is also good for the knife to have a finger guard to protect you from getting cut by the shell.

A selection of oyster knives from our kitchen

Opening Oysters

In order to eat an oyster, one must first remove the top (flat) shell which is connected to the bottom (cupped or deep) shell by a hinge and held closed with a strong muscle. The aim is to snap the hinge and then sever the muscle to get at the goodies inside.

Oysters are most easily opened from the hinge, which is at the pointier end of the shell (Figure 1). To do this, hold the oyster in your left hand (which you should protect with a heavy glove or towel) and the deep shell in your palm. [Alternatively, you can place the oyster on a table and hold it down with your left hand. Naturally, you can switch hands if you're left-handed.] Insert the knife to one side of the hinge, push hard, and give it a twist. If the knife is in deep enough, the hinge will snap and the top shell should pop loose.

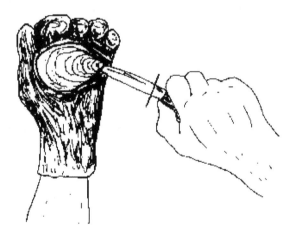

Figure 1. Insert the knife in the hinge and twist

When this is done, slide the knife (Figure 2) along the inside edge of the upper shell to sever the muscle which holds the shells together. Try and cut as close to the upper shell as possible.

While doing this, try not to spill any of the liquor or juice from inside the shell, as this adds to the oyster's flavor.

Figure 2. Slice through the muscle,
without spilling the precious liquid inside

When the upper shell is loose (Figure 3), discard it and pick out any bits of shell with the point of the knife. Finally, sever the muscle below the meat to loosen it from the lower shell.

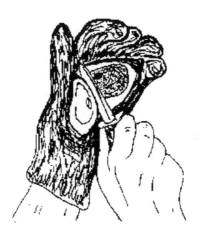

Figure 3. Remove the top shell and
loosen the meat from the bottom shell.

If you can now resist the temptation and not eat this lovely morsel, you can begin to arrange it on a plate or platter or you can read on to see what else you can do with it.

An Easier Way of Getting at the Goodies

If you are going to be cooking your oysters you can, of course make things a little easier for yourself when it comes to getting at the meat locked inside the shell.

Depending on the recipe and your own preference, you can pre-cook the oysters causing the shells to open. The one critical thing here is to bear in mind that you must not over-cook them at this stage as you will be doing the actual cooking later on. If we pre-cook the oysters, we usually stop when we see the first one or two open. Prying the remainder open after this is then quite easy. Pre-cooking the oysters has the added advantage that you can then freeze them for use later on.

These oysters are fresh out of the oven and ready to cook

If you want to prepare just a few oysters, you can put a few into the microwave for a few moments, and they will pop open. You can also put the oysters in the oven or even steam them until they open. The latter two methods are handy for larger amounts of oysters. In the first two cases, place them deep shell down to save the juice. If you steam them in a pot (with very little water), retain the water in the pot for cooking further.

Once they are cooked or used in the recipes that follow, you may freeze the oysters and later reheat as required. This is particularly useful in a busy household or restaurant, or for that long weekend cruising excursion.

Oyster Delight by Jonathan Mite

8.   Fresh Oysters

Oysters on the half-shell

What is the best way to serve fresh oysters? Depending on my mood and appetite, sucked right out of the shell as I'm shucking works just fine for me!

I suppose there are as many different "absolutely correct" methods as there are regions in the world. My own personal favorite is to have them slightly chilled on a bed of fresh seaweed with a piece of lemon and some freshly baked and buttered brown bread.

Other people prefer them on a bed of ice (which I think kills the flavor), garnished with parsley, seaweed, or watercress. Some dribble on hot pepper (Tabasco) sauce, which at times is quite nice. Others use seafood cocktail sauce with horseradish, which seems a pity for such delicately flavored food.

Condiment Suggestions:

- Lemon wedges
- Cocktail sauce
- Hot pepper sauce
- Horseradish

Accompaniment Suggestions:

- Your favorite dry white wine
- Champagne (chilled)
- Stout beer
- 100 proof vodka (chilled)

Whatever way you prefer them is the best way to have them!

Oyster shooters

This is perhaps the only recipe we have here that should really not be served as a main course (for obvious reasons)

- 1 shot frozen 100 proof premium vodka
- 1 raw oyster, shelled
- 1 sprinkle hot pepper sauce

In the summertime, you'll find seaside pubs serving oyster shooters. These can be quite refreshing treats with which to get a party moving. Chill the vodka in the freezer – 100 proof doesn't freeze but it gets syrupy as it chills. Pour a single shot into a double shot glass, add a fresh oyster and a dash of hot pepper sauce. Down it in one swig. Repeat as necessary! And, feel free to experiment with other ingredients.

That's the typical recipe. I prefer to keep the ingredients separate. Eat the oyster, with or without hot sauce. Sip the vodka. You're likely to taste more and remain standing longer this way!

9.   Cooking Oysters

A friend recently lamented my love of cooking oysters stating that it was a shame to spoil them. With a challenge like that, what else could we do but present him with a selection of our favorite recipes. Suffice to say that he too has now 'seen the light' and love oysters in all their appearances.

There are perhaps as many ways of cooking oysters as there are days in the year – probably many more if you get right down to it. Feel free to experiment. If you find something really good, please let us know and we will be pleased to add it to a future edition of this book!

Serving Size

Pretty much all the recipes in the following can be served as appetizers, a first course or as a main course. The serving sizes we mention are often what works best for us and for a given recipe. However you may feel free to modify the quantities as you see fit.

Depending on the size of the oysters, figure on serving up to six fresh oysters per person for a starter, and a dozen or more per person for a full meal. Having said that, we have seen some *C. gigas* oysters that were so huge that a single one would suffice as a full meal. Our cousin quite rightly dubbed these "gaggas".

Breakfast Selection

Some consider the traditional Irish breakfast to be a dozen fresh oysters and a pint of Guinness. Our choice is a fabulously rich omelet that's started on the stove top and browned off under the broiler, forming a frittata -- it beats flipping!

Oyster Frittata

- 24 oysters, shucked
- 3 tablespoons ½ & ½ or cream
- 3 eggs
- 1 stalk celery, sliced thinly
- ½ bell pepper, diced
- 1 shallot chopped
- 2 tablespoons butter
- 1 ounce or more of brandy (optional but very nice)
- Salt and pepper
- Dash of hot pepper
- Handful of grated aged cheddar or Monterey Jack cheese
- A utensil that can go under the broiler, preferably a skillet or a pie tin if your skillets have handles that will melt or catch fire

If you have some giant cupped oysters (gaggers), these do very well here. Just reduce the number of oysters accordingly. Shuck the oysters and chop them into pieces.

39

Melt two tablespoons of butter over medium heat. Toss in the vegetables and cook for a minute. Add the oysters and cook for a minute. Add the brandy and cook for a minute. Beat the eggs lightly together with the cream and the rest of the ingredients. Add to the oysters, reduce the flame/heat to low, and let the eggs set until they thicken. Don't let them get too brown around the bottom. Sprinkle on grated jack or other mild cheese, and then set and lightly brown the top under the broiler.

Magnifique!

Lunch, Dinner and Picnic Selections

Open-Fire Roasted Oysters

- 6+ oysters per person
  more for a main course
- Butter
- Chopped Garlic
- Salt & Pepper
- Baguettes or toast

May induce Warning: eating compulsive behavior

This is one of my very favorites and is also one of the easiest recipes to prepare. It is great as a starter or as a main course for a barbecue. That is why I have been rather vague about the quantities you will require.

For this you will need a good hot wood or charcoal fire and a sheet of metal (cookie tin) to go over it. An old iron frying pan will do for small amounts. This is great for a cookout on a deserted beach.

Heat the sheet of metal on the fire until it is good and hot. Place the unopened oysters on it cupped side down and allow them to roast for 5-6 minutes (possibly a little longer) until they open their shells enough to admit a knife blade. Be very careful when doing this, because many times the oysters will burst open with a miniature explosion sending scalding water and pieces of shell far and wide. Melt the butter in a heat-safe bowl at the end of the sheet of metal, and season to taste with garlic, salt, and pepper.

41

As the oysters open, remove the top shell, cut out the meat, and dip it into the hot butter. Eat as you cook, but don't be surprised at the quantity everyone will consume! The oysters will take on a slight charcoal smoked flavor, which is simply marvelous. Just be careful that you do not leave them on the fire for too long as you do not want to overcook them.

Serve with baguettes (long French bread) or toast.

Grilled Oysters with Garlic Butter and Parmesan

This is a very versatile recipe that you can prepare in any number of ways depending on the ingredients you have to hand.

Serves 4 (main course)

- 4 dozen Oysters (shucked on the half shell)
- 1 pound unsalted butter*
- ½ cup Minced garlic
- Freshly ground black pepper, to taste
- Chopped parsley or chopped shallots (optional)
- 2 cups shredded parmesan*
- 1 baguette

Melt butter in a small pot and add the garlic. Let butter and garlic stand on low heat for about 5 minutes (be careful not to get butter too hot).

Skewered Oysters

- 10 - 12 Oysters
- 2 fluid oz. red wine vinegar
- 1-1/2 teaspoons lemon juice
- 2 tablespoons minced shallots
- 1/2 teaspoon coarsely ground black pepper
- 1/2 teaspoon fresh thyme (optional)
- 16 oz. mixed vegetable (sweet peppers, onions & zucchini)
- Salt and ground pepper to taste

Mix the vinegar, lemon juice shallots pepper and thyme in a shallow baking dish to make a marinade. Rinse the oysters, drain and pat dry. Marinate the oysters in vinegar mixture for 10 minutes.

Skewer vegetables for grilling (skewer like vegetables together for even cooking). Brush vegetables with oil; season with salt and pepper and grill until tender.

When vegetables are almost done, skewer Oysters lengthwise for grilling.

Cook Oysters on grill for 4 minutes. Turn Oysters and cook 4 minutes more, or until oysters are firm when touched. Serve immediately on a bed of grilled vegetables.

Grilled Oysters with Lemon Garlic Butter

Makes 4 to 6 starters or two main courses

- 24 oysters
- 10 tablespoons softened unsalted butter
- 2 tablespoons finely grated Parmesan cheese
- 2 tablespoons minced parsley leaves
- 1 tablespoon lemon juice
- 2 teaspoons minced garlic
- 1 teaspoon minced fresh chives
- 1/2 teaspoon hot sauce, optional
- 1/2 teaspoon salt
- 1/4 teaspoon cayenne pepper

Shuck the oysters leaving the meat in the deep shell.

Combine all ingredients except the oysters in a bowl and mix thoroughly. Transfer butter mixture to a piece of plastic wrap and roll up to form a tight log and freeze until firm.

Preheat a grill to high.

Place the washed oyster shells on a baking sheet and top each shell with 1 oyster. Remove the butter from the freezer and unwrap. Slice the butter into 24 rounds and place 1 round on top of each oyster. Place the oysters on the preheated grill and cook until the oysters are just cooked through, curled around the edges and the butter is melted and bubbly, 4 to 6 minutes.

Serve immediately.

Garlkic Grilled Oysters with Parmesan

Makes 8-12 starters or 4 main courses

- 4 dozen oysters (shucked on the half shell)
- 1 pound unsalted butter*
- ½ cup minced garlic
- 2 cups shredded parmesan**
- 1 French baguette or brown bread

Melt butter in small pot and add the garlic. Let the butter and garlic stand on low heat for about 5 minutes (be careful not to get butter too hot).

Place the oysters in shell on a heated grill (you can also bake them in an oven). If grilling or baking in an oven, place them on a baking sheet or in a shallow pan. Using a ladle or a spoon, drizzle a little of the garlic butter over the oysters. Top the oysters with the cheese and let them cook till juices in the oyster shell start to boil. Slice up the baguette and grill or toast.

Remove oysters and toast bread from the grill and serve.

*   You may also substitute the butter with olive oil

**   Cheese is optional, but very nice. We have used a number of different types of grated cheese, including parmesan, sharp cheddar, cheddar & mozzarella mix or Romano cheese.

A 'single' portion of garlic butter

Grilled Oysters with Spicy Lemon Garlic Butter

- 24 fresh shucked oysters in the half shell
- 8 ounces unsalted, softened butter
- 1 tablespoon minced parsley
- 1 tablespoon fresh lemon zest
- 1 tablespoon cayenne pepper sauce
- 1/2 tablespoon minced garlic
- 2 teaspoons fresh lemon juice
- 1 1/2 teaspoons flake sea salt
- 1/2 teaspoon coarse ground black pepper
- 8 fresh lemon wedges
- 1/2 cup breadcrumbs

Combine softened butter, parsley, lemon zest, cayenne pepper sauce, garlic, lemon juice, sea salt and black pepper in a food processor fitted with a steel blade. Pulse until blended.

46

Spoon this onto parchment paper in a log shape. Roll closed, twisting edges of parchment paper to form a tight log. Refrigerate until firm.

Preheat barbecue grill. Assemble the oysters on a baking sheet or in a shallow pan ensuring that the liquid does not spill out. Top each oyster with 1 slice of spicy lemon garlic butter.

Place the baking sheet on or under the grill and heat for 6 to 10 minutes, or until oysters are bubbling around outer edges; sprinkle 1 teaspoon breadcrumb topping over each oyster.

Remove the oysters from the grill. Garnish with lemon wedges. Serve hot.

Oysters ready to go into the oven or grill

Broiled Oysters

- Oysters on a half-shell
- Worcestershire sauce
- Hot sauce
- Minced bacon
- Minced fresh parsley
- Paprika

Another easy cookout recipe, and this one avoids the potential for exploding shells (but they won't be as juicy).

Preheat broiler or grille.

Open the oysters retaining the fluid in the deeper shell. Arrange them in their half-shells on a cookie sheet. Add 1-2 drops Worcestershire sauce and a drop of hot sauce per oyster.   Sprinkle bacon bits, paprika, and parsley on each.   Broil 4 inches from the flame until edges of oysters just begin to curl and bacon is crisp. If using a BBQ grille, cook bacon until crisp in advance. Fantabulous!

Oysters in Mushroom Caps

Per serving:

- 6 Good-sized mushrooms
- 6 Oyster meats (fresh or canned)
- Salt & Pepper
- Butter

Remove the stalks of the mushrooms and sauté in butter until almost tender. Place a mushroom, cup side up, in a well greased shallow pan. Put an oyster in each cup, season with salt and pepper, and add a small pat of butter. Bake in a 400° F oven until the edges of the oysters curl.

Oysters Française

- 2 dozen oysters on the half shell
- 4 ounces Brie cheese
- 2 tablespoons chopped pimento
- Lemon slices or wedges

Preheat oven to 450°.

Open oysters and leave on half-shell. Top each oyster with a thin layer of cheese. Garnish with chopped pimento. Bake for about 10 minutes, until cheese is melted and oysters are plump. Serve with lemon slices.

Oysters Vinaigrette

Per serving:

- 6 Pre-cooked and chilled oyster meats
- ½ Cup mild onions, minced (we like Vidalia)
- 6 Olives, sliced
- Lettuce (Romaine or Boston are our favorites)
- Olive oil
- Vinegar (balsamic can be used)
- Chopped basil
- Chopped parsley

Arrange the oysters on a bed of fresh lettuce and top with onions and olives. Mix the oil (2/3) and vinegar (1/3). Add the parsley and basil. Shake well, and pour over the salad. Serve cold.

Elegant and simply delicious.

Oysters Rockefeller

Per serving:

- 6 Freshly opened oysters
- ¼ cup chopped spinach
- ¼ clove chopped garlic
- 2 Tbsp chopped scallions or chives
- 4 Tbsp butter
- 1 Tsp chopped parsley
- ¼ Tsp lemon juice
- ¼ Tsp Worcestershire sauce
- 2 Tbsp breadcrumbs
- Pernod, Absinthe, Anisette, or Arrack
- Salt & Pepper

Put the finely chopped spinach, onions, parsley, and garlic into a bowl and salt and pepper lightly. Sprinkle in the lemon juice, Worcestershire sauce and bread crumbs. Add a few drops of Pernod or similar flavoring. Soften and work in the butter. Transfer to a saucepan and gently sauté the sauce over a low heat.

Pace opened oysters in a baking pan and bake for about 5 minutes at 450° F, or until the edges of the oysters begin to curl. Quickly put a generous tablespoon of the green butter sauce over each oyster and return to the opver to bake for a further 5 minutes. Do not allow the oysters to brown.

Serve alone as an appetizer, or for a main course serve with brown bread and tomato salad, or some red and yellow pepper salad.

Angels on Horseback

(or Astronauts on Piggyback)

Per serving:

Warning:
May induce compulsive eating behavior

- 6 Oysters
- 3 Slices of bacon*
- Lemon
- Parsley, chopped
- Garlic, very finely chopped or pressed
- Pepper

Wrap half a slice of bacon around each oyster meat and skewer with a wooden toothpick. Place wrapped oysters in their deep shells in a shallow baking pan. Add a squeeze of lemon, and spice with a touch of garlic and a grind of pepper. Grill over a hot fire until bacon is cooked. This can also be done under the grill in an oven, but the meats must be turned to cook the bacon thoroughly.

Sprinkle on some parsley and serve with warm fresh brown bread.

*   Streaky bacon and not lean back bacon

Champagne Poached Oysters

- 2 dozen fresh oysters on the half shell
- 2/3 cup oyster liquor
- ½ cup champagne (or dry white wine)
- 2 shallots, minced
- Dash of salt and a pinch of pepper
- 1 bunch watercress, trimmed

Combine all ingredients and cook over medium heat only until oysters are plumped. Do not boil. Remove oysters with slotted spoon. Spoon a bit of liquid into each shell. Garnish with watercress and serve immediately.

Potato Crusted Oysters

Delightful as an appetizer or a first course

- 6 large oysters
- 1 egg
- 1 Tablespoon water
- 1/2 cup all-purpose flour
- 1/2 cup instant mashed potato flakes
- 4 Tablespoon butter

Carefully shuck the oysters, remove the meat, and discard the upper shells. Warm the lower cup-shaped shells. Pat the oysters dry on paper towels.

Add the water to the egg and beat. Dredge the oysters first in the flour, then in the egg mixture, and finally in the potato flakes.

In a nonstick sauté pan, heat the butter until it is sizzling. Quickly add the oysters and brown them first on one side, then the other. Remove them from the pan, and briefly place them on a paper towel. Transfer the oysters to their shells and serve immediately.

Fried Oysters

Fried oysters are a southern American delicacy and are often an ingredient in many other recipes. Here's a basic way to prepare this traditional feast.

- 1 pint shucked oysters, drained
  (save the liquor for another time)
- 1 cup all purpose flour
- 1 cup fine bread crumbs
- 2 eggs
- 2 Tbsp light cream
- 1 tsp salt
- Freshly ground pepper
- 1 stick (8 Tbsp) butter
- 1 cup vegetable oil (Canola or corn)

Mix flour and breadcrumbs on waxed paper. Season with salt and pepper. Beat eggs with cream in a shallow dish. Pat oysters dry with a paper towel. Roll oysters in flour/bread crumb mixture, then dip in egg mixture, then in crumbs again. Make sure they're coated thoroughly. (Hint: chilling the oysters in a refrigerator while preparing the next step will help the coating set so it doesn't fall apart when fried.)

Heat butter and oil in a large skillet until just sizzling. Reduce heat. Fry oysters in batches until nicely browned, 2-3 minutes on a side. Do not overcook. Remove oysters from skillet and drain on paper towels.

Serve with lemon wedges and tartar sauce with a side of French fries and salad. Fried oysters also go extremely well with the likes of a Caesar salad.

Oyster Po Boy

Per serving

- 4-6 fried oysters (see preceding recipe)
- French bread (baguette)
- Lettuce, tomatoes, pickles, etc.
- Sliced cheese
- Mayonnaise, mustard, gravy, etc.

Slice the bread along one side so that it folds open like a book. Cook the oysters in your favorite manner; fried as in the preceding is a favorite of ours. Open the bread and add the cheese, shredded lettuce, and oyster meats. Add condiments to your liking. Close the bread (as you would a book) and mash it down.

Po Boy

'Po boy' is southern US slang for "poor boy". This is what the sandwiches that were traditionally given to the poor street boys by the nuns in New Orleans were called. It is basically a New Orleans sandwich similar to the "sub" sandwich. They can be made with anything, but are typically made with a type of meat and "dressing" (lettuce, tomatoes, pickles, and sauce). Mother's Restaurant in New Orleans is well-known for their debris po' boy, made with the "debris" from a roast that falls into gravy when a roast is cut.

Other main ingredients may include: thinly sliced meat (ham, turkey, roast beef, etc.), shredded pork, spaghetti bolognaise sauce (also called a Sloppy Joe), fried seafood (shrimp, oysters, fish, etc.), you name it.

Hangtown Fry

Serves 3 to 4

- 8 Oysters
- 4 slices bacon cut in 1-inch pieces
- 2 oz. flour, + 1 oz. cup of bread crumbs-combined
- Beat 8 eggs
- 1/3 teaspoon salt
- Dash of pepper

Fry bacon until crisp. Remove from pan. Drain Oysters and roll in flour crumb mixture. Fry in bacon fat over moderate heat; cook two minutes each side. Place bacon pieces over oysters and cover with beaten egg mixture. Lift Oysters to let egg mixture flow to bottom of the pan. Cover pan and fry over low heat until eggs are cooked.

Serve hot, with parsley and lemon wedge.

Pan-fried Oysters in Corn Flour

Serves 3 to 5

- 6 Oysters
- 4 oz. corn flour
- 2 eggs, beaten with 1 teaspoon water
- 2 tablespoons vegetable oil or cooking oil

Drain Oysters. Dip prepared Oysters in egg, then in corn flour, coating thoroughly. Set aside to dry.

Heat oil or fat in frying pan to 370 degrees Fahrenheit (or until quite hot). Fry Oysters until golden brown on one side, then turn carefully to brown the other side (about 4 minutes on each side).

Serve immediately.

Lazy Oyster Fry

...Or Oysters, Shaken not Stirred

Goes great with a dry vodka martini!

Follow the cooking instructions as for fried oysters, but instead of the flour and bread crumb and egg mixtures, simply coat the oysters in prepared dry pancake mix. The easy way is to put some mix into a plastic bag, season it, drop in the oysters and shake. Clean up couldn't be easier! Just dispose of the bag when you're done.

Irish Oyster Fritters

Per serving:

- 6 Oysters
- 1 Tbsp Flour
- 1 Egg
- 3 Tsp melted butter
- 3 Tbsp oyster juice
- 1 Tsp chopped parsley
- Vegetable oil
- Sliced lemon
- Tartar Sauce

Stiffly beat the egg and fold in the flour, oyster juice, and butter. Let this set for two hours. Dip the oyster meats into the batter. Deep fry and drain. Sprinkle with parsley, and serve with lemon slices and tartar sauce. A side of fresh corn on the cob goes really well.

Sketrick Island Fritters

Serves 3-4 as a starter, 2 as a main course

- 20 medium oysters
- 1 cup bread crumbs
- 1 tablespoon mint, fresh, chopped
- 1 tablespoon thyme, fresh, chopped
- 1 tablespoon marjoram, fresh, chopped
- 1 tablespoon oregano, fresh, chopped
- 1 tablespoon shallots, fresh, chopped
- 1 tablespoon parsley, fresh, chopped
- 2 tablespoons flour
- 3 large eggs
- 1 tablespoon butter
- 1 tablespoon olive oil

Shuck the oysters and remove from their shells. Drain in a strainer set over a bowl. Mix the breadcrumbs together with the spices, and salt and pepper (to taste). Place this mixture in a shallow dish.

Whip the eggs and place in another shallow dish. Heat the butter and olive oil in a pan, on medium heat. Olive oil and butter tend to burn easily, so be careful not to have the heat too high. Dip the oysters one by one in the flour. Dip into the beaten eggs. Dredge each oyster in the breadcrumb mixture and place in the pan of heated oil and butter. Cook the oysters over medium heat until crisp and golden brown on one side. Turn and cook on other side.

Serve with a salad of your choice

Daria's Oyster fritters

- 6 Oysters - chopped
- Course flour
- Chopped onions
- 1 Egg yolk
- Salt & pepper

Combine chopped oysters with, egg yolk, some course flour, salt & pepper until just right consistency to form patties. Fry in olive oil till slightly brown on outside. Serve with Pickapeppa sauce.   Also works great with many other shellfish!

Oyster Casserole

Makes 4 servings

- 1 pt Stewing oysters (canned or freshly shucked)
- 1/4 c Butter
- Salt; to taste Pepper; to taste
- Cracker crumbs
- 1 Egg; beaten

Preheat oven to 350 degree. Butter the casserole dish. Layer casserole with half the oysters, dot with butter. Season with salt & pepper; sprinkle with crumbs. Repeat the above. Pour egg over all. Bake 30 minutes or until done.

Oysters Mornay

Per serving:

- 6 Oysters
- 2 Tbsp butter
- 1 Tbsp flour
- ¼ Cup milk or cream
- 2 Tbsp oyster liquor
- 3 Tbsp grated Swiss cheese
- 1 Tbsp Parmesan cheese
- Worcestershire sauce
- Lemon juice
- Salt & Pepper
- Cayenne pepper

Open oysters, retaining the oyster juice. Melt the butter in a saucepan and stir in the flour until the mixture is well blended. Add the oyster juice and cream (or milk) and then fold in the cheese, retaining a little. Add a few drops of Worcestershire sauce and some lemon juice with salt and pepper to taste. Mix in the oysters, and then return the oysters with sauce back into their shells. Now sprinkle with grated cheese and cayenne pepper. Bake or grill until the tops are golden brown.

Serve with brown bread or toast.

Oysters Vera

Per serving:

- 6 Oysters
- 2 Tbsp Oyster juice
- 2 Tbsp butter
- 1 Tbsp capers, chopped
- 2 Tbsp cream
- 2 Tbsp bread crumbs
- ¼ Cup chopped celery
- 1 Tbsp Flour
- Salt & Pepper

Sauté the oysters and celery in one tablespoon of butter for three minutes. Add the capers and oyster juice and stir in the cream. When the cream is heated, remove half of the sauce into a small bowl and gradually add the flour. Stir until the flour is dissolved. Return this to the saucepan and stir until it thickens. Spoon the oysters and sauce into cleaned oyster shells. Melt the remaining butter and add the bread crumbs. Pour this over the oysters. Bake or grill until golden brown.

Serve with brown bread or toast.

Peace Maker

- 4 Italian bread rolls
- 8 slices bacon
- 1/2 pint (8 ounces shucked oysters, drained and patted dry)
- Flour
- salt and pepper
- 2 medium tomatoes, chunked
- 1/2 cup sour cream
- 1 teaspoon horseradish

Slice off the very top of the rolls and scoop out soft bread inside to form a shell.

Fry bacon until crisp. Remove and drain on paper towels. Season flour with salt and pepper. Dredge oysters in flour (Those poor oysters get dredged one way or another!). Fry in bacon fat until browned on both sides. Remove and keep warm. Cook tomato chunks in remaining bacon fat until heated through, 10-15 minutes. Place cooked bacon, oysters and tomatoes in bread shells. Mix sour cream and horseradish and serve as a sauce.

Waterman's Oyster Pie

- 1 pint oysters
- 2 small potatoes, diced
- 1 stalk celery, sliced
- 1 carrot, sliced
- 1 small onion, chopped
- 2 Tbsp butter
- 2 Tbsp oyster liquor
- ¼ cup warm half & half or cream
- salt & pepper to taste
- pinch of Cayenne pepper
- 2 favorite recipe pie crusts (top & bottom)

Drain oysters, reserve liquid. Boil potatoes and drain. Sauté celery, carrots and onions until almost tender. Prepare pastry, divide in half, and line 9 inch pie pan. Alternate layers of oysters and vegetables. Salt and pepper each layer, sprinkle with Cayenne and dot with melted butter. Mix oyster liquor and warm cream, and pour over contents of pie. Add top crust, and slit to vent. Brush top with lightly beaten egg white if desired for a beautiful golden-brown sheen. Bake at 450 degrees for 10 minutes. Reduce to 375 degrees for 30-35 minutes.

Sautéed Oyster and Spinach Salad

Serves 3-4

- 10 - 12 Oysters
- 4 slices bacon
- 2 tablespoons red wine vinegar
- 3 teaspoons Dijon mustard
- 5 tablespoons olive oil
- 1 tablespoon bacon drippings
- 8 oz. cleaned and torn spinach leaves, loosely packed
- small onion, chopped finely
- Ground pepper to taste
- 8 slices French bread, rubbed with garlic and toasted

Cut bacon into 1-inch pieces, sauté until crisp. Drain bacon on paper towel. Pour off bacon drippings and reserve. Remove pan from heat.

Whisk together vinegar, mustard, oil and 2 teaspoons bacon drippings for dressing, set aside.

Rinse oysters, drain and pat dry. Return pan to heat. Add 1 teaspoon of the bacon drippings and Oysters. Sauté for 8 minutes, or until Oysters are golden brown and firm to the touch.

Place Oysters on a bed of spinach and green onions.

Sprinkle on the bacon and dressing. Add ground pepper to taste and serve with garlic toast.

Oyster Linguine with Carrots and Zucchini

- 10 - 12 Oysters
- 8 ounces of dry, uncooked linguine
- 2 tablespoons olive oil
- 6 garlic cloves, peeled and smashed
- 2 oz. julienne carrots
- 2 oz. julienne zucchini
- medium glass dry white wine
- 4 teaspoons fresh chopped parsley
- 1 teaspoon grated orange peel
- Salt and ground pepper to taste

Rinse oysters, drain and pat dry.

Bring water to a boil for pasta. Cook according to package directions.

In a large skillet, heat oil. Sauté garlic until lightly browned. Add Oysters, carrots and zucchini. Sauté 8 minutes or until Oysters are golden brown and firm to the touch.

Add wine and remaining ingredients. Simmer two minutes. Serve immediately over cooked pasta.

Deviled Oysters

- 12 well-cleaned oysters with deep shells
- Cayenne pepper to taste
- 2 hard-boiled egg yolks
- 2 raw egg yolks
- 1 teaspoon fresh lemon juice
- 1 tablespoon melted butter
- Salt to taste
- 2 tablespoons toasted bread crumbs
- 12 sprigs fresh thyme

Preheat oven to 350 degrees. Open the oysters and sprinkle with cayenne. In small bowl, mash hard-boiled yolks. Mix in raw yolks, lemon juice, butter, and salt. Spoon mixture over oysters, then cover with bread crumbs. Bake on cookie sheet for 5 minutes, or until bread crumbs are toasted. Garnish with thyme.

Oyster Loaves

- 3 small loaves French bread (baguettes)
- 1/2 teaspoon garlic powder
- 2 tablespoons melted butter
- 3 dozen fresh oysters
- 2 tablespoons melted butter
- Milk

Almost split the loaves lengthwise, leaving a hinge. Scoop out the soft middle and save the crumbs. Then add a 1/2 tsp of garlic powder (not salt) to 2 tablespoons melted butter, and brush the cavities.

Drain the oysters and save the liquid. Sauté them in the rest of the butter till the edges curl (about 5 minutes). Put the oysters into the loaves, mix the crumbs you saved with the oyster liquid you saved, and add them, too. Shut up the loaves now. Then wrap them in cheesecloth dipped in milk, twisting the ends and tucking them under the loaf. Bake them on a baking sheet for half an hour at 350 degrees. Cut them in half before you serve them.

Carpetbag Steak - Oyster Surf & Turf

This is a uniquely Australian dish that was first popularized in Sydney around 1950.

- 1 thickly cut fillet steak
- 3-4 oysters
- Worcestershire sauce

Optional
- limes
- Shredded cheese
- lemon juice

Cut a small pocket, approximately 6cm (2.5") in length and about the same depth, in the edge of the steak. Dip the oysters into the Worcestershire sauce, and then place them in the pocket in the steak.

Now you can optionally add lime pulp, some shredded cheese or a squeeze of lemon juice into the pocket.

Seal the pocket with a moistened skewer and cook over a moderate heat in a heavy based frying pan.

Oyster Stuffing - a different take on Surf & Turf

(for a 12-pound bird)

- 16 oz. bread crumbs
- 2 oz. melted butter
- 3 oz. finely diced celery
- medium finely diced onion
- 1 egg well beaten
- Salt and Pepper to taste
- 8 Oysters

Sauté the celery and onion lightly in butter. Cut each Oyster into 1/2 - inch pieces. Mix all ingredients thoroughly. Stull fowl, and roast.

Oysters Kilpatrick

Per serving

- Finely chopped bacon
- 6 oysters
- Tomato sauce
- Worcestershire sauce
- Lemon wedges (optional)

To begin you need to make the Kilpatrick sauce which is 1 part Tomato Sauce to 1 part Worcestershire Sauce which is thoroughly mixed together.

Open the oysters and generously sprinkle with bacon. Pour the Kilpatrick sauce over the top of the oysters and bacon. Now the oysters can be placed in an oven proof frying pan with a stable base for the oysters.

Bake at 350 degrees until the oysters are firm to the touch and bacon is crispy. The oysters can also be placed in a tray under a grill with a high heat until firm and bacon is crispy.

Serve the Kilpatrick oysters with either lemon wedges or additional Kilpatrick sauce.

Roasted Oysters with Madeira

Serves 4

- 24 oysters (or 50 small oysters)
- 1/4 stick butter
- 1/2 cup Madeira wine
- Salt and cayenne pepper to taste

Roast the unopened (cleaned) oysters in their shells in a large pot over medium high heat until they open up and have started to dry out, but are not scorched.

Remove the oysters from the shell onto a plate, without any of the remaining liquor. Discard any oysters that failed to open.

Melt the butter in a pan on low heat. Add the oysters heating them up without sautéing them. Add the Madeira, a little salt and cayenne. Serve when the wine sauce is hot.

10. Soups and Stews

These can be starters or main courses

Easy Cream of Oyster and Mushroom Stew

This one you can even make aboard a cruising sailboat! It's one of my favorite uses for cream of mushroom soup. Try the golden mushroom variety for a twist.

Makes about 5-6 cups

- 1 pint oysters
- Oyster liquor
- 4 tablespoons butter
- 1/2 cup sliced celery
- 1/2 cup chopped onion
- 1/2 cup diced carrots
- 1 10.5 ounce can cream of mushroom soup
- 1/2 cup milk
- 1/4 cup chopped parsley
- 1/4 teaspoon white pepper

Melt butter in a two-quart saucepan. Sauté celery, onion and carrots in melted butter until lightly cooked, about 5 minutes. Add liquor that has been drained from oysters. Add mushroom soup and milk; stir until smooth. Heat until it simmers but doesn't boil. Add parsley, oysters and white pepper. Heat until oysters are plump and edges begin to ruffle. Serve immediately.

75

Traditional Maryland Oyster She-Stew

Makes about 6 cups

- 1 pint shucked oysters, with liquor
- 1 quart milk
- 1/4 cup (1/2 stick) margarine or butter
- 1 stalk celery, sliced
- salt and pepper to taste
- Old Bay seafood seasoning, if desired

Cook oysters in their liquor ever so slightly over low heat until edges of oysters just begin to curl. Cook celery lightly in melted butter, just to flavor the butter. Do not allow the butter to brown. Remove celery. Add milk and butter to the oysters stirring constantly. Salt and pepper to taste. Heat slowly until hot; do not boil. For an extra zip, sprinkle seafood seasoning on each serving.

The she-stew is considered a great opening course but a bit too feeble as a main course for the working man. See He-Stew recipe.

Traditional Maryland Oyster He-Stew

Simply the most beautifully presented recipe ever

"'You cain't tell a she arster from a he,'...'I ain't talkin' about the arsters, I'se talkin' about the eaters.' He smiled benignly at the watermen and asked, 'What's it to be, she or he?'"

From James A. Michener's "Chesapeake", Copyrighted in 1978 by Random House, Inc., Chapter 22, "The Waterman"

(The preceding and following are an excerpted conversation between the cook, Big Jimbo and the crew aboard the Skipjack, Jessie T. as she prepared for her maiden trip to dredge for "arsters" in Maryland's Choptank River)

- A "mess" of bacon (several slices)
- Oil
- 8 large onions
- 2 stalks celery
- 48 oysters, shucked
- Liquor from 48 oysters
- 1 Quart of milk
- Some cream
- Sprinkle of tapioca powder
- Dusting of saffron
- ½ pound of butter

"A he-stew was something quite different, and Big Jimbo mumbled to himself as he prepared his version,

77

'First we takes a mess of bacon and fries it crisp.' As he did this he smelled the aroma and satisfied himself that Steed's had sold him the best. As it sizzled he chopped eight large onions and two hefty stalks of celery, holding them back till the bacon was done. Deftly he whisked the bacon out and put it aside, tossing the vegetables into the hot oil to sauté. Soon he withdrew them, too, placing them with the bacon. Then he tossed the forty-eight oysters into the pan, browning them just a little to implant a flavor, then quickly he poured in the liquor from the oysters and allowed them to cook until their gills wrinkled.

Other ship's cooks followed the recipe this far, but now Big Jimbo did the two things that made his he-stew unforgettable. From a precious package purchased from McCormick Spice Company on the dock in Baltimore, he produced first a canister of tapioca powder. 'Best thing ever invented for cooks' in his opinion. Taking a surprisingly small pinch of the whitish powder, he tossed it into the milk, which was about to simmer, and in a few minutes the moisture and the heat had expanded the finely ground tapioca powder into a very large translucent, gelatinous mass. When he was satisfied with the progress he poured the oysters into the milk, tossed in the vegetables, then crumbled the bacon between his fingers, throwing it on top.

The sturdy dish was almost ready, but not quite. From the McCormick package he brought out a packet of saffron, which he dusted over the stew, giving it the golden richness augmented by the half-pound of butter he threw in at the last moment. This melted as he

78

brought the concoction to the table, so that when the men dug in, they found before them one of the richest, tastiest stews a marine cook had ever devised.

'Do we eat this good every day?' Caveny asked, and Big Jimbo replied, 'You brings me the materials, I brings you the dishes.'"

Break crackers into bowls and spoon the gloriously rich mixture on top.

Be sure to thank the Lord for your bounty. Amen.

Meike's Oyster Bisque

- 6 Oysters
- Sliced onions
- Chicken stock
- Salt & pepper

Saute some sliced onions in butter. Add chicken stock (fish stock is too fishy). Add oysters for just a tiny while. Blend all in a blender, but not too fine. Add salt & pepper to taste.

Oyster Chowda

The difference between chowda (=chowder) and stew is that chowda is thicker. Some say you have to be able to stand your spoon up in it!

Makes about 5-6 cups

- 3 tablespoons butter
- 2 tablespoons flour
- 3 cups milk or half & half
- 2 cups fresh oysters and liquid
- 1/2 teaspoon chopped dill
- 1/4 teaspoon salt
- 1/8 teaspoon white pepper

Make a roux by melting 1 tablespoon of butter over medium heat, adding the flour and cooking until barely browned. Add milk gradually and stir until hot, but never boiling. Drain the oysters and heat their liquid separately to a boil. Melt remaining butter and lightly sauté oysters until they plump. Add heated milk to the sautéed oysters. Stir and serve at once in heated bowls. Add a splash of sherry right before serving.

Oyster Stew - Recipe 1

- 8 oysters
- 8 fluid oz. milk
- 1 pint light cream
- 2 tablespoons butter
- Dash cayenne pepper
- Salt and pepper to taste

Heat milk and cream together until film shimmers over surface. Do Not Boil.

Drain Oysters. Add Oysters (sliced if you prefer), and butter to hot milk and cream mixture. Heat, but do not boil, for five minutes more. Add seasonings and serve at once.

Oyster Stew - Recipe 2

- 24 oysters (fresh or canned)
- 1/4 cup cream
- 1 tablespoon butter
- 1 tablespoon flour
- salt, mace, and pepper, to taste

Shuck the oysters saving any liquid. Stir flour into the cream. Melt the butter in a pan and add the oysters and their liquor. When they become hot, stir in the cream and flour. Season to taste with salt, mace, and pepper. They should be served as soon as they are taken off the fire.

Oyster Stew - Recipe 3

- 24 oysters (fresh or canned)
- 2 ounces butter
- 1/4 cup cream
- 1/4 teaspoon mace
- 2 bay leaves
- Salt, black pepper, nutmeg, to taste.

Shuck the oysters saving any liquid. Put your oysters with all their liquor into a saucepan. Add the butter, salt, black pepper, mace, and bay leaves. Bring to a simmer for five minutes. Add the cream and stir all well together while heating through.

Pour onto a plate or platter. Sprinkle a little fresh nutmeg on each oyster as it lies in the sauce. Serve immediately.

11. Uses for Oyster Shells

Historically, oyster shells were used as a form of currency. Nowadays most of us simply discard the empty shells when we're done feasting. Apart from the traditional creation of a kitchen midden for historical purposes (a lucky archeologist will dig it up some day and be able to study its contents), there are a variety of other modern-day applications for oyster shells.

"And there it was, the Chesapeake! In Pentaquod's language the name meant: the great river in which fish with hard shell coverings abound, and each village along the Susquehanna possessed precious lengths of roanoke made from these white shells gathered from the Chesapeake. With enough roanoke a man could purchase even a chieftain's daughter."

"This was the river of rivers, where the fish wore precious shells."

From Chesapeake, By James A. Michener

In some communities (in Florida for example), crushed oyster shells are used in place of gravel or blacktop for paving driveways. They look great, permit good drainage, stay cooler under hot sun, and are easy to obtain. Then every time you eat oysters, you just toss them onto the driveway. How efficient!

Shells are also used for making calcium supplements. So the wonderful creature not only satisfies our silver palate, it also helps us prevent osteoporosis. However, personal experience has shown, that the shells are quite hard and not easy to chew. They need to first be pulverized, and there are pharmaceutical factories specialized in doing this. Getting them to the pharmaceutical manufacturer is not always the easiest thing to accomplish, though.

But did you think of all those other things that these wondrous shells can be used for in your own back yard? You can create wonderful crafts with your children or grandchildren. Oyster shells are also useful for creating jewelry, with mother of pearl being highly prized in many countries. Not only is it used in jewelry, but also for inlaid wood furniture, and decorative arts like lampshades. A simple wind chime can provide hours of entertainment in the making and years of proud reflection thereafter. All it takes is a drill, some string, and a trip to the ImagiNation®. That same wind chime can be magically transformed into a scarecrow for your boat. By simply hanging it from the spreaders or other high point, you can chase away all those nasty poop machines from the deck, saving hours of clean-up labor!

Crushed oyster fragments can be added to your compost heap, where they will then add calcium to your soil, and help with the drainage of water.

The best way to recycle the shells is to return them to the seabed where permitted. Here they may provide a suitable surface for future generations of oysters to settle on.

We'd love to hear about other uses for oyster shells for future editions. Send your ideas, and your recipes (we'll give you full credit for any published in future editions).

And happy oystering to you!

12. Acknowledgements

I've been collecting these recipes for a long time. Unfortunately, I cannot recall exactly who passed on which recipes to me. There were many people who sent me newspaper clippings and some, such as Toke Stevens, June Quinberger, and Kirstin MacDonagh, gave me their own recipes with their roots in Clew Bay, Ireland. Some were acquired during travels to far-away islands while others were born by the mighty Chesapeake Bay. Many of these were edited, combined, or refined to present to you in this issue of the Oyster Delight Collection. I thank all who contributed and apologize for any oversights.

A particular thanks to those patient souls who made this text legible. I hope you will enjoy the end result – I certainly have...

Jonathan Mite

Oyster Delight by Jonathan Mite

13. Post Script

You'll notice that many of the recipes suggest serving the oysters with brown bread. That's a very Irish tradition. Just in case you can't find a good hearty brown bread, here's a recipe for you to try, courtesy of Kirstin MacDonagh, owner of the renowned seafood restaurant, Quay Cottage, in Westport, Ireland. We're also throwing in two tartar sauce recipes in case you're off cruising the Pacific and don't have access to the good prepared brands like McCormick's and Crosse & Blackwell's.

Our Brown Bread

Originally from Miriam Moore

- 1 lb coarse whole meal stone ground flour
- ½ lb pinhead oatmeal
- 2 tsp bread soda
- 2 tsp salt
- knob of butter
- 1 pt buttermilk

Mix all together. Spoon into 2 greased 1 lb loaf tins. Bake in hot oven (gas 5) for 35 min (or more in my oven).

If you happen to be traveling or for that matter are at home and in need of tartar sauce, but without access to the proper ingredients, there are alternatives:

Home Made Tartar Sauce

- 2 hard-boiled eggs
- 1 egg yolk, raw
- 1 cup olive oil
- 1-2 tablespoons red wine or balsamic vinegar
- 2 tablespoons chopped parsley
- 2 tablespoons chopped chives
- 2 tablespoons chopped pickles and/or capers

Scoop the cooked yolks out of the eggs and beat them with the raw yolk in a blender (or with a mixer). Dribble the oil bit by bit as you blend until the sauce thickens. Add the vinegar to taste. Remove the sauce from the blender and stir in the other ingredients.

You can chop the cooked egg whites and use them as a savory topping for many dishes including fried oysters.

Simple and Quick Tartar Sauce

- 1 half cup good quality Mayonnaise
- 1 tablespoon creamy horseradish sauce
- 1 tablespoon chopped sweet peppers
- 1 tablespoons chopped pickles and/or capers
- add dill, salt and pepper to taste

Simply mix the ingredients and you will be surprised at the positive comments you get from around the table.

Oyster Delight by Jonathan Mite

92

14.   About White Seahorse and the ImagiNation™

The ImagiNation™ is:

Where dreams take flight and become reality...

White Seahorse focuses on publishing books for and about marine subjects and anything else we take a fancy to. We are proud and pleased to provide this edition of Oyster Delight.

White Seahorse is a division of Knowledge Clinic Limited, Port Aleria, Rosnakilly, Kilmeena, Westport, Co. Mayo, Ireland

Legend of the White Seahorse

In old seafarers' lore, white crested waves frothing with foam were said to be white seahorses riding on the surface for all to see, perchance carrying Poseidon's forces. Under the conditions when the waves raised these creatures out of the sea, performance of the ship and its crew had to be at its peak while being fully tested by the elements.

It was such a strong image that the O'Malley clan in the west of Ireland, from their seafaring stronghold in Clew Bay in today's County Mayo, adopted a white seahorse as the symbol of their prowess in the often challenging waters of the Atlantic. With it, they infused their clan with strength on land and sea...Terra Marique Potens.

Granuaile, or Grace O'Malley, the infamous 16th century female privateer who sailed up the Thames to negotiate with Queen Elizabeth, was said to ride a white horse on land and flew the White Seahorse flag at sea aboard her vessel, Moytura.

In tribute to Grace and in memory of Major M. Joseph O'Malley Blackwell, past chief of the O'Malley Clan, we named our publishing business White Seahorse. We intend to carry on the tradition of strength on land and sea with exceptional service to the sailing cruisers of this world. May the white seahorses carry you safely to your destination.

For more on Ireland, visit:

http://www.discoverireland.ie
http://www.coastalboating.net (our site for boaters)

15. Also Available from White Seahorse

Happy Hooking - The Art of Anchoring

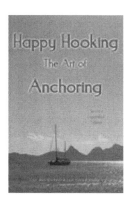

Happy Hooking is a very readable book loaded with valuable information on anchoring tackle, anchoring technique, tying up and rafting, anchoring etiquette, as well as the occasional anecdote - simply stated a must have! (If we don't say so ourselves)

The second expanded edition of Happy Hooking - the Art of Anchoring features:

- More gear
- More photos
- More illustrations
- More independent reviews
- Experience from both sides of the Atlantic
- Personal anecdotes based on thousands of miles of sailing and countless times anchoring

Happy Hooking is available from amazon.com and coastalboating.net

Happy Hooking Reviews

Stu Hochron "News From The Bow"

Before going any further, let me refer you what I consider to be the best available reference on anchoring, ""Happy Hooking", by Alex and Daria Blackwell, Published 2008 by White Seahorse, Inc. The Blackwells detail all aspects of anchoring in this inexpensive paperback volume, and include the newest technology in anchors and technique. If you read this book before you head out, and you will be better prepared for any anchoring challenge.

Latitude 38

We've often wondered why anchoring, one of the most common and important acts of cruising, is often done so cluelessly. One reason might be the stodgy and impenetrable tomes that have been written on the subject over the years. Thankfully, this isn't one of them. Happy Hooking — the Art of Anchoring is well organized, well illustrated, user friendly in its delivery, and even fun — authors Alex and Daria Blackwell even tell you the proper way to organize one of those round 'sunflower' raft-ups. Reading just a few pertinent chapters in this easy-to-understand book will not only 'clue you in', but help guarantee that your boat will still be there when you come back from a trip ashore.

Latitudes & Attitudes Seafaring Magazine

For those who sail, there is one thing that is pretty well a rule of thumb. You will have to anchor, and if you know the secrets, it isn't all that hard. The authors give you their insight into the secrets of anchoring in most situations, allowing you to avoid the embarrassing moments when your anchor doesn't do what it's supposed to.

Sail-World.com

If there's one thing that the cruising sailor needs to know well, it's how to anchor! When overnight at anchor, you'll sleep well if you know that the anchor is secured and you're not going to find yourself out to sea or, worse (the nightmare scenario), be woken in the dark by the noise of the rudder bouncing on a rocky shore. So the answer is to have every skill at your disposal, and this new book by the Blackwells contains a wealth of information. The book is readable and interesting, and has plenty of illustrations and diagrams. It might be compulsory reading for the new sailor, but even the most experienced will find much new material here.

Happy Hooking is available from amazon.com and coastalboating.net

16.   A Parting Thought

"As I ate the oysters with their strong taste of the sea and their faint metallic taste that the cold white wine washed away, leaving only the sea taste and the succulent texture, and as I drank their cold liquid from each shell and washed it down with the crisp taste of the wine, I lost the empty feeling and began to be happy and to make plans."

A Moveable Feast, **Ernest Hemingway**

Thank you and may the wind and sea be kind to you!

Your Friend on Land or at Sea

Jonathan Mite

99

7156195R00062

Printed in Great Britain
by Amazon.co.uk, Ltd.,
Marston Gate.